D0607181

NATURE WATCH

BABOONS

Written by
Melissa Stewart

Lerner Publications Company • Minneapolis

Text copyright © 2007 by Melissa Stewart

Lerner Publications Company
A division of Lerner Publishing Group
241 First Avenue North
Minneapolis, Minnesota 55401 U.S.A.

Website address: www.lernerbooks.com

Library of Congress Cataloging-in-Publication Data

Stewart, Melissa.
    Baboons / by Melissa Stewart.
      p.   cm. — (Nature watch)
    Includes bibliographical references and index.
    ISBN-13: 978-1-57505-868-9 (lib. bdg. : alk. paper)
    ISBN-10: 1-57505-868-5 (lib. bdg. : alk. paper)
    1. Baboons—Juvenile literature. I. Title.
  QL737.P93S745 2007
  599.8'65—dc22   2006018967

Manufactured in the United States of America
1 2 3 4 5 6 – DP – 12 11 10 09 08 07

CONTENTS

Baboons, like these olive baboons above and on page 5, often take afternoon naps in trees.

BABOON BASICS

AS THE SIZZLING MIDDAY SUN BEATS DOWN ON AN African plain, a pride of lions snoozes lazily in the open grass. Not far away, large groups of zebras and gazelles graze nervously. A leopard rests on the lowest branch of a lone tree, while vultures fight for the final scraps of an early morning kill. A small herd of elephants slowly saunters by. They are headed toward the river, where hippos lounge in the shallow water. It is quiet and peaceful.

After a busy morning of searching for food, a **troop** of olive baboons naps in the trees along the river. But one lively youngster can't get to sleep. He climbs down and begins exploring. The little baboon's movements don't go unnoticed. A hungry crocodile watches him. As the baboon wanders closer and closer to the water's edge, the croc quietly

Baboons have free-moving arms and legs, flexible fingers, and front-facing eyes.

monkeys—lives in the tropical rain forests of Central and South America.

Both Old World monkeys and New World monkeys are members of an even larger group called **primates**. The first primates evolved about 65 million years ago. These creatures were similar to the lemurs, lorises, and tarsiers alive today.

Baboons are the largest monkeys in the world, but they are not the largest primates. That honor belongs to the great apes (orangutans, gorillas, bonobos, and chimpanzees) and humans.

All primates have many traits in common. From fist-sized galagos to 400-pound (180 kg) gorillas, all 240 **species**, or kinds, of primates have arms and legs that can move freely. They all have flexi-

Just as the crocodile is about to attack, a series of short, sharp barks shatters the silence. It is the alarm cry of a female baboon. She has just awakened and realized her youngster is in trouble. Without a moment's hesitation, a nearby male races to the ground, scoops up the little one, and carries him back to safety. It was a close call.

Dramas like this one have been playing themselves out for millions of years in the grasslands of Africa. According to scientists, the first baboons lived on Earth about 12 million years ago. They are members of a group called the Old World monkeys. All Old World monkeys live in Asia and Africa. Another group of monkeys—the New World

Like this olive baboon, all baboons have bare faces and long snouts.

ble fingers and toes, eyes that face forward, and large brains.

Many primates, including baboons, have excellent eyesight. They see the world in a full range of vivid colors and can judge distances accurately. And they have thumbs set opposite their four other fingers. These **opposable thumbs** let them grab and hold objects.

Baboons walk on all four limbs and have thick, furry coats. They have large heads and long snouts with two small nostrils at the tip. A baboon's face is bare. Its small, close-set eyes are almost hidden below heavy brow ridges that protect them from the sun's harsh rays.

Baboons are active during the day and sleep at night. They usually sleep sitting upright on rocks or tree branches. Leathery buttock pads on their backsides help baboons stay balanced on their nighttime perches.

Baboons have leathery buttock pads to help them stay on tree branches.

Male baboons are larger and heavier than females. Males have long bushy hairs on their heads and shoulders.

Adult male baboons have a mane, or cape, of long silky hair on their head, neck, and shoulders. They are about 3 feet (1 m) tall and weigh between 50 to 110 pounds (25–50 kg). Females do not have a mane. They are a little shorter than males and only half as heavy.

Scientists divide baboons into five separate species based on how they look, how they act, and where they live. Olive baboons (*Papio anubis*) have greenish olive coats and live in a band of land that runs across the middle of Africa. Most live on grassy plains with a few scattered trees. These plains are called **savannas.** They also live in open woodlands. Yellow baboons (*Papio cynocephalus*) are slightly smaller and have yellowish brown fur. Their **home range** overlaps with the olive baboon's and extends to the south. They are also most common in savannas and open woodlands.

Chacma baboons (*Papio ursinus*) are a little larger than olive baboons. Their fur is yellowish gray, brown, or black. They live mostly in the grassy savannas and open woodlands of southern Africa. Guinea baboons, also known as western baboons *(Papio papio),* are the smallest members of the baboon family. They have reddish brown coats and live in savannas, open woodlands, and rocky regions of western Africa.

Top: **Chacma baboons live on the savannas of southern Africa.** *Bottom:* **This group of yellow baboons includes a large male, two females, and a baby.**

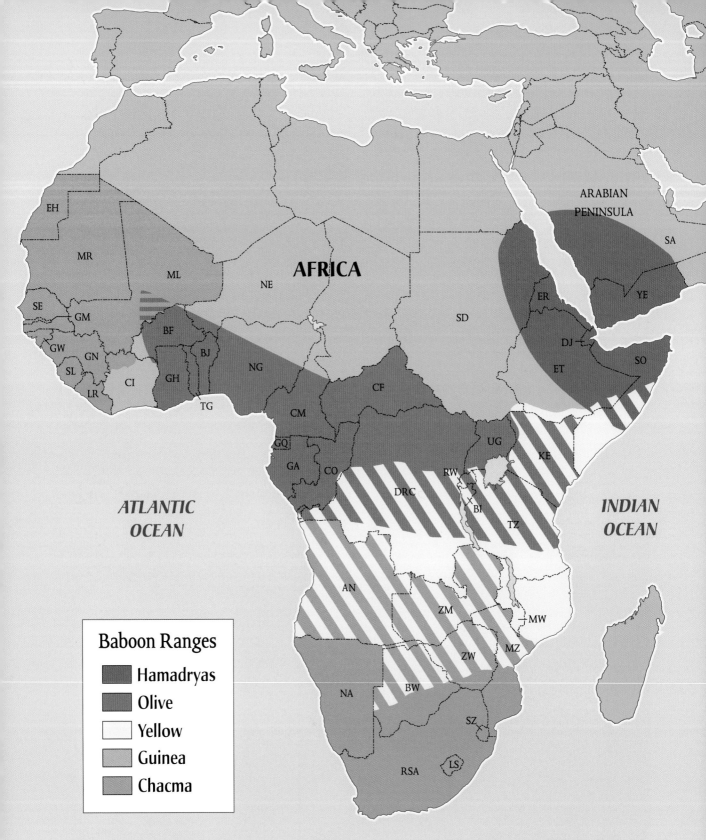

Baboon Ranges

- Hamadryas
- Olive
- Yellow
- Guinea
- Chacma

Most baboons live in the open woodlands of central and southern Africa. Only the hamadryas baboons live in the dry areas of eastern Africa and on the Arabian Peninsula. And only the guinea baboons are in western Africa.

Hamadryas baboons (*Papio hamadryas*) have a very different **habitat** from that of their relatives. They live on dry plains and rocky outcrops in northeastern Africa and in the southwestern part of the Arabian Peninsula. Males have long, thick, gray fur. The females' fur is brown.

Guinea baboons are the smallest members of the baboon family. They live only in western Africa.

Hamadryas baboons live in dry, rocky places in northeastern Africa and the southwestern Arabian Peninsula.

A Day in the Life

AT THE FIRST RAYS OF MORNING SUNLIGHT, BABOONS shake themselves awake and lick the morning dew off their fur. They climb down from the trees where they slept all night and grunt to one another in greeting. Then they sit in small groups and **groom** one another. During grooming, one baboon picks insects, dirt, and bits of dead skin out of another baboon's fur. But grooming is more than just a way to stay clean. It is a way of expressing friendship and establishing trust.

After grooming, the baboons spread out to search for food. When they find fruit, grasses, flowers, roots, or seeds they like, they stuff them into their cheek pouches. Then they move on.

This chacma baboon has found a water lily for its meal.

As the baboons search for more tasty treats, they use their tongues to move small amounts of the stored plant material from their cheeks into their mouths. Then they grind it slowly with their powerful back teeth.

Baboons spend most of their days foraging, or searching for food. They have large bodies and live in places where food can be hard to find. They often travel about 5 miles (8 km) a day to get enough to eat. Their flexible arms and opposable thumbs help them in their search. Because baboons are intelligent, they can use a variety of methods to get food. They pick leaves and berries and scoop plant roots out of the ground. They use rocks to crack open nuts and pound wild wheat against rocks until the grains fall out.

But sometimes baboons need more **nutrients** than plants can provide. Then they use their hands to catch fish, gather birds' eggs, hunt for worms and snails under rocks, and peel bark off trees in search of insects. Once in a while, an adult baboon may even manage to catch a lizard or a bird. When baboons are very hungry, several males may work together to kill a rabbit, a baby antelope, or a smaller monkey. Then the whole troop shares the meal. Baboons use their long, sharp canine teeth to rip and slice the **prey** into bite-size chunks.

Just like you, a baboon has thirty-two teeth. The incisors at the front of its mouth are perfect for biting leaves and stems off plants and grabbing chunks of meat. A baboon uses its long, sharp canine teeth to rip and slice meat. The wide, flat premolars and molars at the back of a baboon's mouth crush and grind plant materials.

In the late afternoon, the baboons spend some more time foraging. But by early evening, the troop has settled near their nighttime sleeping trees. While the adults groom one another, the youngsters do somersaults, wrestle, and chase one another around.

A male yellow baboon feeds on a young gazelle.

In the middle of the day, when the blazing sun is high overhead, most baboons nap. If they stumble upon a clump of trees, they will climb into them for their afternoon snooze. But if not, they will just stop wherever they are. While a few baboons act as lookouts, the rest of the troop sit down, drop their heads, and fall asleep.

A chacma troop searches for food in the grasses under a tree.

As night falls on the African savanna, the baboons climb into the trees and carefully balance their bodies on the outermost branches. Here they will be safe from leopards and other **predators.** The baboons curl their toes tightly around the tree branches, close their eyes, and drift off to sleep.

Yellow baboons settle down for the night high in a tree.

17

INSIDE
THE TROOP

MOST BABOONS LIVE IN TROOPS. SOME BABOON TROOPS
are about the same size as a large human family. Others have as many
as two hundred members. Most troops contain about fifty animals. The
baboons in a troop eat, sleep, work, and play together. They protect
one another from danger, and they comfort one another when times
are tough.

A typical baboon troop might include seven to ten adult males, four-
teen to twenty adult females, and twenty to thirty youngsters. The oldest members of a troop are usually around 30 years old, but some
baboons may live as long as 45 years. A female baboon usually has her
first baby when she is about 6 years old, so a 30-year-old female could
be a great-great-great-grandmother.

Most of the females in a troop are related. They are mothers, daughters, sisters, and aunts. Sometimes a troop includes two or three families of females that have lived together for many years. The females in a troop form close friendships and usually remain in the group for their entire lives.

In each generation of baboons, some females have a higher **rank**, or place within the group, than others. When an old female dies, the family rank is passed on to her oldest daughter. She takes over her mother's role within the troop.

The oldest baboons with the highest rank are accepted as the group's female leaders. When the troop faces a crisis, such as a shortage of food or water during a drought, younger baboons expect the wise old females to solve the problem. The old-timers have been around the longest. They are most likely to remember how the troop dealt with similar emergencies in the past.

When male baboons are about 4 years old, they leave their troop and search for a new one. They need to find a different group so that when they are fully grown, they can mate with females that are not their close relatives.

Left: A male olive baboon grooms a female to show he is a friend.
Below: Baboons often form close friendships within the troop.

A male olive baboon grooms a female while she grooms a youngster. A lower-ranking male may find a place in the troop by helping a female.

A young male will not find it easy to join a new troop. At first, larger, stronger males challenge newcomers to fights and try to chase them away. To be accepted into the group, a young male must win over the females first. He can show his good intentions by grooming the females, sharing food with them, and helping care for their babies. When a mother baboon seems tired, a young male can volunteer to carry her baby. When a predator or baboon bully threatens a youngster, the newcomer can defend it. After a while, the helpful, new male will be accepted as a full member of the troop.

But this doesn't mean his troubles are over. Next, he must earn a rank within the troop. Because the males in a baboon troop are not related, their ranks cannot be passed down from generation to generation. Young males must try to climb the troop's social ladder by fighting or outsmarting higher-ranking members.

How a male ranks in the baboon society is important. Rank determines how much nutritious meat a male gets to eat. And rank among baboons is a lot like popularity among humans. Female baboons are usually most attracted to strong, dominant males with high ranks.

Two male baboons fight over rank in the troop.

Males may also fight over shares of meat.

Most young male baboons devote a lot of time and energy to challenging higher-ranking males so they can improve their social status. But they must also keep an eye on lower-ranking males who might want to challenge them. Often the male ranked number three in a troop will spend a lot of time harassing number two. He will try to steal food from the higher-ranking male or take over his sleeping spot. As number three gets bolder, he may even try to prevent number two from grooming or mating. Meanwhile, baboon number four will be breathing down number three's neck, trying to move himself up a step in the troop's ranking.

Fighting among males is common within baboon troops. Sometimes all that bickering takes its toll on the entire group. The highest-ranking males, the troop's male leaders, have many important responsibilities. It is their job to lead the troop as it travels each day. They must always be on the lookout for predators. They must make sure youngsters do not stray from the group. If dominant males are constantly fighting, the troop will have less time to look for food each day. They may be more open to attacks by leopards, lions, and other enemies.

Baboon troops are healthiest and happiest when the top male has a long, peaceful reign and can keep other high-ranking males in check. The cleverest male baboons become and remain dominant not by winning fights but by avoiding them. A good leader must win the loyalty, trust, respect, and friendship of both male and female members. He must choose his battles carefully.

A top-ranking male, like this olive baboon, is responsible for leading the troop.

Baboon
Relationships

THE WAY TWO BABOONS ACT WHEN THEY MEET SHOWS how they feel about one another. When females greet their children, their female relatives, or the males they like, the baboons usually touch noses, smack their lips, and grunt softly. They may even hug.

When two males greet one another, their actions reflect their rank and their willingness to cooperate. If a young male is looking for an ally, he stands upright. He walks rapidly toward his intended partner with a rolling stride. Then he looks directly at the other male and flashes a let's-make-nice smile like the hamadryas above. He may also use other friendly gestures, such as smacking his lips, flattening his ears back, and narrowing his eyes.

If the second male is feeling friendly, he maintains eye contact and smacks his lips in return. Then the two males may give one another a quick hug or nuzzle. To complete the greeting, each animal lets the other one touch his private parts. This shows that the males trust one another and want to cooperate. As soon as the greeting is complete, both males walk away.

If the second baboon is not interested in friendship, he usually just turns around and walks away. But if he feels agitated, he may stare angrily, raise his eyebrows, bob his head, and grind his teeth. This is not a good sign. The first baboon usually smiles and slowly backs away. But if he feels offended, the two males may begin to circle one another warily, each one jockeying for the dominant role in the greeting. The baboons may end up getting into a minor scuffle or an all-out fight.

At meeting, two rival chacma baboons challenge each other.

A male chacma baboon communicates a threat with a yawn.

According to scientists, the complexity of baboon greetings shows that baboons are very intelligent animals. That is not the only way baboons use their brains. They have developed dozens of different calls for communicating with one another. They also often cooperate while feeding and defending themselves from predators. These clever creatures have even learned how to unzip researchers' tents to steal food stored inside.

Friendly greetings are more common among older males who have known one another for many years. For these old-timers, forging partnerships is often the best way to get a mate. Two or more older males will try to drive off a younger, more dominant male. This will give one of them a chance to woo a female. The older males are willing to put themselves in harm's way because they know that their friend will return the favor.

Scientists who study baboons in the wild say that this strategy works. They have observed older males mating at least as often as socially dominant younger males. Sometimes they mate more often than the younger males. Scientists have also noted that the older males who have the most success with the females are the ones that complete the most "trust greetings" with other males.

This is not the only time when a female's choice in mates is based on something other than a male's rank. When it comes to attracting a female, friendship often outweighs fierceness. According to scientists, a female usually chooses mates that have lived in the troop for 3 to 5 years. They are males who have spent time grooming her, eating with her, and interacting with her children.

Fighting for a high rank isn't always the best way to get a female's attention. While male number two is battling it out with number three, lowly number eight may sneak in and try to woo the female. He's been her friend for years. Sometimes being nice is better than having a high rank.

A yellow baboon female grooms the male of her choice.

A friendly middle-ranked male may find a good life in the troop.

Middle-ranking, friendly males may also have a better life when they get older. When a top-ranking male finally loses a fight, the younger generation of rough, tough males doesn't let him forget it. They beat him up whenever they get a chance. If things get bad enough, the defeated male may even decide to leave the troop.

Old age is certainly no time for an animal to spend alone on the savanna. By the time a baboon is in his late 20s, his senses are dimmer and his muscles are weak. Predators lurk everywhere. But sometimes the danger seems preferable to constant abuse from younger males. If the older male manages to join a new troop, younger males will probably leave him alone. They will quickly realize that he isn't a threat.

But sometimes a defeated male decides to remain in the troop and tough it out. When this happens, it's usually because over the years he developed close friendships with a few of the females in the troop. He often groomed them, and they groomed him in return. When one of these female friends felt sad or upset, the male sat close and offered her comfort. The male played with his female friends' youngsters and made sure they did not stray too far from the group.

If a male baboon develops these kinds of friendships throughout his adult life, he will be rewarded during old age. Older females will continue to be his friends. Some younger females will choose him as a mate because they recognize him as an important member of the baboon community.

A group of yellow baboons takes care of one another.

ANOTHER WAY OF LIFE

HAMADRYAS BABOONS LOOK VERY SIMILAR TO THEIR baboon relatives, but they live in a very different habitat. And they lead a very different kind of life. While most baboon troops have at most two hundred animals, hamadryas troops may have as many as eight hundred members. These huge troops do not have the same kind of close-knit community spirit as other baboon troops. The animals come together in the early evening and share a sleeping site, but they do not spend all their time together.

Every morning, the large hamadryas troop breaks up into smaller groups called **bands**. Each band is about the same size as a typical troop of olive or yellow baboons. The band functions in a very similar way too. The members of a hamadryas band travel and feed together, and they

Each hamadryas baboon band is made up of several **clans**. Most of the time, the males in a clan are very closely related. Unlike other male baboons, male hamadryas usually stay close to their fathers, uncles, sons, brothers, and grandfathers. It is the females that move from one group to another. As a result, male hamadryas are much more likely than other male baboons to groom one another, defend one another from enemies, and share food.

A hamadryas clan includes related males.

Two hamadryas baboons greet each other.

A clan is divided into two or three family groups called **harems**. A harem consists of one adult male leader, two to eleven adult females, and their youngsters. When young females are old enough to mate, they leave their harem and their clan and search for a new group to join.

When most males are fully grown, they leave their harem and move around freely within their clan. They try to attract or kidnap females from other harems so they can start a family of their own. Some young males remain with their harem or join a different harem in their clan as followers. The followers help the male leader find food and protect the harem, but they are not allowed to mate with any of the females.

When a male leader grows old, he may allow one or two loyal followers to mate with the females, as long as they do not challenge his authority. Eventually, the old male lets his most devoted young follower take his place as the group's leader.

Even though male hamadryas have all the power, females do have ranks. The female with the highest rank spends the most time with the male leader and mates with him most often. But if she misbehaves or lags behind when the group is moving, she will get the same punishment as any other female—a swift kick in the butt or a sharp bite on the neck.

Female hamadryas baboons leave their clans when they are old enough to mate and raise young.

Hamadryas males don't have to waste time worrying about their social status. They can focus most of their attention on keeping their group safe and finding food. This is very important because the hamadryas's dry, desertlike home is a hard place in which to survive.

Hamadryas must spend nearly all their time foraging. They usually travel more than 6 miles (10 km) each day in search of food and water. That's farther than any other primate must go to get the nutrients it needs.

A young hamadryas baboon stays close to its mother while she is foraging.

Hamadryas males cooperate to keep the clan safe and well fed.

RAISING A FAMILY

FEMALE BABOONS ARE READY TO START A FAMILY WHEN they are about 5 years old. Male baboons usually start looking for mates when they are around 7 years old.

Male baboons know when a female is ready to mate because her rear end swells up and turns bright pink. If the female has a high rank, many males will try to woo her. Over her lifetime, the high-ranking female will probably give birth to more babies than lower-ranking females. More of her youngsters will survive to adulthood too.

A middle-ranking female is usually approached by two or three males. She chooses one, and about 6 months later, a tiny baby is born. Like human babies, baboon infants are born throughout the year. But olive, yellow, and chacma mothers give birth most often between October and December,

A newborn baboon weighs 1 to 2 pounds (0.5–1 kg) and is covered with thick black fur. As the baby grows, the color and texture of its coat slowly changes until the little one looks just like its parents.

During a baby baboon's first month of life, it stays very close to its mother. Like other female **mammals**, a mother baboon makes rich, nutritious milk inside her body and feeds it to her baby. At night, the mother and baby sleep cuddled together. During the day, the mother carries the baby next to her stomach as the troop moves. She uses one arm to hold her youngster and the other to gather her food.

By the time a baboon is 5 or 6 weeks old, it can walk by itself. But it still can't move fast enough to keep up with the troop. When it is time to forage, a mother baboon bends her back legs and lowers her body so her youngster can climb onto her back. Then she raises her tail to brace the baby's back, so it won't fall off.

Opposite page: Baboon babies are born with thick black fur, but it begins to lighten in just a few weeks.
Above: When a baby baboon is small, its mother carries it next to her stomach.
Right: The babies nurse, or drink mother's milk, for about eight months.

At first, a young baboon wraps its arms and legs around its mother's body and clings tightly. But soon it learns to sit up straight and enjoy the ride. As the troop travels, the youngster pays close attention to everything it sees. It learns how to act and what to eat by copying its mother. The two baboons often communicate with soft clicking and chattering noises.

When a youngster is 4 to 6 months old, it begins to spend more and more time with other young baboons. While the adults groom and search for food, the youngsters play. They run and tumble and wrestle. Like human children, they seem to enjoy a good game of hide-and-seek, tag, or king of the mountain. If these games get too rough or a bully goes too far, watchful adults come and restore order.

By the time a baboon is about 8 months old, it has usually stopped drinking its mother's milk. The young baboon knows how to find its own food and has no trouble keeping up with the troop. Soon the youngster will be old enough to take care of itself, and its mother can have another baby.

Top: **An older baby rides on its mother's back.**
Bottom: **Young olive baboons spend their time in play.**

Most female baboons give birth to a new baby every two years. Having just one baby at a time means that the little one gets all its mom's attention. When baby baboons are well fed and cared for, they are more likely to survive to adulthood.

WHY BABOONS HAVE SURVIVED

YOUNG BABOONS ARE SMALL, CURIOUS, AND PLAYFUL, so they can be an easy target for hungry predators. That's why their mothers and other adults in the troop are always on the lookout for danger. But adult baboons don't have many natural enemies.

At night, they take great care to choose a place where they will be safe from leopards. During the day, their keen senses of sight and smell usually warn them of prowling predators. If a baboon detects an approaching leopard, lion, or cheetah, it belts out an alarm bark. Then the entire troop scurries to the highest branches of the tallest trees. Because Africa's big cats are so much larger and heavier, they cannot go out on the smaller branches and reach the clever baboons.

If a predator catches a troop by surprise, the baboons mob it and scream to scare it. If the big cat continues to threaten the group, the troop's male baboons attack it with their sharp, flesh-tearing teeth. If the predator doesn't flee quickly, it may be seriously wounded.

When the attack is over, the baboons return to their daily activities. They forage and feed until their stomachs are full. Then they amble to a sleeping site and groom until the sun goes down.

Threats from enemies are a normal part of life on the savanna. Baboons have managed to survive on Earth for millions of years by developing a lifestyle that gives them everything they need to survive.

Recently, however, baboons have had to face a new enemy—humans. Baboons have learned the hard way that people aren't deterred by mobbing or sharp teeth. Guns and other human weapons are far superior to a baboon's built-in defenses.

A heavy leopard can't reach the small branches where a baboon can find safety.

Even though people don't often hunt baboons, the animals have learned the best ways to escape from human attacks. Instead of clambering up the nearest tree, they flee into the thick undergrowth, where they can't be seen.

Baboons have also learned that while some humans can be dangerous, most are not. Over time, they have figured out ways to live alongside humans. They are the animals most likely to walk within a few feet of tourists on safari at Africa's **wildlife sanctuaries.** And they know that farmers' fields can be a good place to sneak a snack. As long as they don't stay too long or eat too much, the farmers will not harm them. Baboons adapt well and can live just about anywhere. As a result, they adjust even when their original habitat is taken over or lost.

Baboons also have another advantage. They seem to be able to understand humans' intentions. This has allowed scientists to learn much about baboons. Researchers have discovered that if they approach a troop slowly and in a non-threatening way, they can get very close to baboons and watch them interact.

These chacma baboons have no fear of the humans on safari.

Scientists think that baboon families and relationships may be similar to those of early humans.

Scientists have spent days, weeks, and even months following troops. As a result, they have learned where they go, what they eat, and how their societies work.

Most researchers think that our earliest human ancestors lived in the savannas and open woodlands of Africa—the same habitat in which baboons are found. Because baboons are among our closest relatives, scientists believe that their lifestyle and relationships may be very similar to those of the first humans. So by studying baboons, we may be able to learn more about ourselves and our past.

GLOSSARY

bands: a group of hamadryas baboon clans that lives together. A hamadryas band is as large as a troop of other baboon species. A hamadryas troop includes many bands.

clans: in hamadryas baboons, extended family groupings. A clan usually consists of two to three harems.

groom: to pick insects, dirt, and bits of dead skin out of another animal's fur. For many animals, grooming is also a way of expressing affection and establishing trust.

habitat: the area where an animal or plant lives, grows, and reproduces

harems: in hamadryas baboons, family units that include one male leader, several females who mate with only the male, and their young

home range: the territory in which a particular animal lives

mammals: animal that have a backbone and hair and feed their young mother's milk

nutrients: substances, especially in food, that are needed for healthy growth

opposable thumbs: thumbs that are set opposite the other four fingers. Having hands with opposable thumbs makes it easier to grasp and hold food and other objects.

predators: animals that hunt and eat other animals

prey: an animal that is killed and eaten by other animals

primates: the group of mammals that includes lemurs, lorises, tarsiers, galagos, monkeys, great apes, and humans. All primates have flexible fingers and toes and arms and legs that can move freely. They have large brains and forward-facing eyes that can judge distances accurately.

rank: a baboon's status, or place, within its group. Rank usually determines a baboon's access to food and opportunities to mate.

savannas: land areas covered with grass and scattered trees

species: a group of organisms that shares certain characteristics and can mate and produce healthy young

troop: a group of baboons that lives together

wildlife sanctuaries: areas set aside by governments or private groups where animals are protected from human hunters

SELECTED BIBLIOGRAPHY

Barrett, Louise. *Baboons: Survivors of the African Continent*. New York: DK, 2001.

Estes, Richard D. *The Safari Companion: A Guide to Watching African Mammals*. White Junction River, VT: Chelsea Green Publishing Company, 1999, pp. 405–409.

Nowak, Robert M. *Walker's Mammals of the World*, 6th ed. Baltimore: Johns Hopkins University Press, 1999, 588–590.

Sapolsky, Robert M. *A Primate's Memoir: A Neuroscientist's Unconventional Life among the Baboons*. New York: Scribner, 2002.

Strum, Shirley C. *Almost Home: A Journey into the World of Baboons*. Chicago: University of Chicago Press, 2001.

The author spent July and August 1996 in Kenya and Tanzania, where she observed baboons and learned about their habits.

An olive baboon mother grooms her baby.

FURTHER READING

Churchman, Deborah. "The Adventures of Curious Bobby: How Baboons Spend Their Day." *Ranger Rick*, January 2002.

Horak, Steven A. *Baboons and Other Old World Monkeys*. Chicago: WorldBook, 2002.

Lockwood, Sophie. *Baboons*. Chanhassen, MN: The Child's World, 2005.

WEBSITES

Canadian Museum of Nature, Ottawa, Ontario. "Baboons."
National History Notebooks.
http://www.nature.ca/notebooks/English/baboon.htm
This site features a brief description of the baboon with illustrations.

Conservation Corporation Africa. "Savannah Baboons—Life in the Troop."
Wildwatch.
http://www.wildwatch.com/resources/mammals/baboon.asp
This site provides photos and detailed information about the natural history of the various savanna baboons of Africa

Out to Africa with Ellen and Paul (Jansson). "Baboons."
http://www.outtoafrica.nl/animals/engbaboon.html
Written by frequent travelers to Africa, this website includes information from the African Wildlife Foundation about African animals, including baboons.

INDEX

ABOUT THE AUTHOR

While on safari in Kenya and Tanzania, **Melissa Stewart** saw many troops of olive baboons. During the day, they often crisscrossed the dirt roads, blocking tourists' jeeps. When they felt tired, they simply stopped wherever they were, dropped their heads, and took a short power nap.

Stewart has always been fascinated by the natural world and is a careful observer. Before becoming a full-time writer, she earned a bachelor's degree in biology from Union College and a master's degree in science and environmental journalism from New York University. She then spent a decade working as a science editor.

Stewart has written more than a seventy children's books about animals, ecosystems, earth science, and space science. She has also contributed articles to *Ask, Click, Highlights for Children, National Geographic World, Northern Woodlands, Odyssey, Ranger Rick, Science World, Wildlife Conservation*, and *ZooGoer*. Stewart lives in Acton, Massachusetts. You can visit her website at www.melissa-stewart.com.

PHOTO ACKNOWLEDGMENTS

The images in this book are used with the permission of: Image Source Royalty Free by Getty Images, all backgrounds, pp. 1, 5, 13, 15, 18, 24, 26, 30, 36, 39, 40, 44, 45, 46, 47, 48; © Sergio Pitamitz/Robert Harding World Imagery/Getty Images, pp. 2-3; PhotoDisc Royalty Free by Getty Images, pp. 4, 18, 31, 33; © Mitch Reardon/Lonely Planet Images, pp. 5, 45; © David A. Northcott/CORBIS, pp. 6 (top), 12, 24; © Mary Ann McDonald/CORBIS, p. 6 (bottom); © Rob and Ann Simpson/Visuals Unlimited, p. 7; © Eric and David Hosking/CORBIS, p. 8; © kevinschafer.com, p. 9 (top); © Jonathan & Angela Scott/The Image Bank/Getty Images, p. 9 (bottom); © Gerald Tang, p. 11; © Kennan Ward/CORBIS, p. 13; © Nigel J. Dennis; Gallo Images/CORBIS, pp. 14, 16 (right), 40; © Carol Polich/Lonely Planet Images, p. 15; © Kevin Schafer/CORBIS, p. 16 (left); © age fotostock/SuperStock, pp. 17, 27, 29; © Joe McDonald/CORBIS, p. 19 (inset); © Ariadne Van Zandbergen/Lonely Planet Images, p. 19 (bottom); © Jonathan & Angela Scott/Taxi/Getty Images, p. 20; © C & M Denis-Huot/Peter Arnold, Inc., pp. 21, 22; © James P. Rowan, p. 23; © Frans Lemmens/Iconica/Getty Images, p. 25; © Andrew Parkinson/Lonely Planet Images, p. 26; © Adrian Bailey/Lonely Planet Images, p. 28; © Stuart Westmorland/CORBIS, p. 30; © Joseph Van Os/The Image Bank/Getty Images, p. 32; © Uwe Walz/CORBIS, p. 34; © SuperStock, Inc./SuperStock, p. 35; © Gallo Images/CORBIS, pp. 36, 37 (top left); © Sally A. Morgan; Ecoscene/CORBIS, p. 37 (bottom right); © Martin Harvey/CORBIS, p. 38 (top left); © Brian A. Vikander/CORBIS, p. 38 (bottom right); © James Warwick/The Image Bank/Getty Images, p. 39; © Tom Brakefield/CORBIS, pp. 41, 43; © Darrell Gulin/CORBIS, p. 42.

Front and back cover: Image Source Royalty Free by Getty Images.